A Simple Guide

To

Investing

in

Turnaround Stocks

How to Successfully Invest in
Stocks of Turnaround Companies

Table of Contents

Table of Contents

Preface

When a company is headed in the wrong financial direction and they want to reverse course, this is considered a turnaround situation. A company on this path often doesn't see the light at the end of the tunnel.

It may or may not be the company's fault. Outside factors such as an unexpected law suit or increased government regulation could put a strain on cash reserves.

As an investor, you can take advantage of a turnaround situation if you know what to look for. There are opportunities to participate in a turnaround situation that often times are not as drastic as a company heading into bankruptcy.

Some turnaround situations rise from short-term events such as a mistake in the direction the company took. As an example, maybe a company opened a new store... only to find out unexpectedly that a major highway was going to be built next to it.

The highway project significantly cut down consumer traffic that was very high when the feasibility study was undertaken. Or maybe management just calculated wrong and the store was not profitable. Nonetheless, after investors sell the stock after blaming management, the stock could be sitting at an attractive price.

In this eBook I will be exploring the investment potentials of turnaround stocks from various perspectives from identifying, buying and of course managing them.

CHAPTER 1

Investments - Why Invest In stocks?

Stocks are considered to be a good investment opportunity for several reasons. The key to remember is that stocks are not typically a fast turnaround for earning money. If you have several years to invest and wait for the return, stocks can be a good investment choice for you.

Stocks typically have a higher rate of return on the investment over time than other opportunities such as real estate or bonds. There are several good benefits to investing in stocks for the future, whether the goal is to have college tuition or retirement money when the time comes.

Benefits to stock investments include:

Higher rates of return- over time, stocks often outperform other investments such as CDs or real estate.

Taxes- if the stocks are held in the investment for over a year, the profits upon selling are only taxed 15%, which is the long term capital gains tax rate. This rate is lower than the standard rate of taxing.

Diversification- investing in stocks can be part of a diversified portfolio. The investment funds can be divided among several solid stocks such as blue chip stocks and the like. By keeping a diversified portfolio, the investor minimizes the risks.

Diversification helps keep the portfolio stable even as stocks go up and down.

If stocks are not an investment method that appeals, there are many other options that are good options but might not have the solid rate of return or the lower taxes upon cashing in.

Those who wish to keep their investments liquid and accessible might opt for savings accounts or online savings accounts where the interest rates are good yet the money is accessible without penalty if it were to be needed. Stocks can be sold at various times to liquidate funds, the penalties or lower return rates subject to the particular circumstance and arrangements of the stock purchase agreement.

Investments are a part of a solid financial plan for the future. They are a great way to put aside money that will grow to be accessed in the future. These are funds that can be used for college tuitions, wedding expenses or retirement income or supplement.

While there are many people who would prefer to simply put cash into a savings account, investments done carefully and knowledgably are often worth the effort as the returns can be substantial.

Some research and talking with experience investors can lead new investors to the best stocks in which to invest.For more information on investing in investment opportunities usually or normally not found in the marketplace.

Basic approach to stocks

In this chapter I am going to offer a few thoughts on what I believe helps me to be successful and a few examples of what can and may go wrong. As ever, I hope that this isn't below your level of either confidence or competence as I don't wish to insult.

However, I have found that there seem to be far more people that want to understand finance 'a little better' than there are people who can lecture on the subject.

Firstly to an example. Back in the late 90's I joined an Investment club in the UK. I knew a couple of the members from a local health club I was a member at. Knowing that I was (a) keenly interested in investment and (b) more knowledgeable than most of them, I was invited along.

Suffice to say that on the first evening, I realised that I had been invited along to do all the work! I enjoyed the work so that didn't actually bother me. I also could purchase some additional investment tools 'for the club' which I couldn't justify for myself.

The main work of analysis was carried out by myself and another member who is a long-time friend and no mug in the world of shares and investment himself. We were using as our template a theory offered by Jim Slater which centred around price / earnings growth ratios. In short, it was highly successful.

At the end of the first year, we were 'up' by around 80%. Admittedly, this was during the tech-boom bull and any idiot could get 30% pa without trouble or effort, but still we were very impressed.

The second year started well too and within 6 months of year two, our small company growth share portfolio (the only portfolio) was up comfortably over 100%. Nice work if you can get it.

For those of you that haven't been a member of an investment club and don't know, they are a democracy. Every opinion counts equal in a vote to buy or sell, whether they understand investment - or not.

Here was our trouble. If you can believe it, making an enormous profit was 'boring' and they needed 'excitement'. To me, making money as quickly as we did was not merely exciting - it was thrilling!! But, when we wanted to sell they wouldn't and when we offered rock solid buy predictions they disliked something and again, we wouldn't.

I think our lowest point was not buying shares in a UK pizza delivery firm (that was growing very quickly and would have turned into a great investment) because (and I kid you not) one of the founding members didn't like 'Italian food'. Who cares?

The club ended rather badly with arguments and falling outs. Several years later it still has a couple of holdings in shares that might 'one day turn around'. Fat chance!!!!

So here is the tip: why do you want to invest? This needs analysis.

My friend and I invested because we were willing to put in the effort, wanted to increase our holdings, make money and frankly, we like winning in a global market against the nation's smartest minds!!

Our other members however, were there to gamble. It was just fun. Who cares about the result? We all meet in a pub, have a meal, chat about shares and throw some money at the market. We wanted profits, they wanted a social group.

After being up by over 100% after 18 months, we closed the club at a loss of both money and friendship. Ridiculous.

What about you? Why do you want to invest? If you want to gamble, take up sports betting. You get to watch a game as well as be financially involved - that sounds much better.

Do you plan to follow the market? If you don't, best to keep away.

I'm not the world's greatest at tracking a market - I can admit it. Each day, I look at the shares in my portfolio, funds I advise clients about, prospective investments I am mulling over, general financial news and read a few posts by other advisers / analysts online.

And yet, if I'm honest, I worry that don't pay enough time each day to the markets.

If you want to make serious decisions, with serious amounts of money and (hopefully) make serious amounts of profit, you need to be - SERIOUS!!!

Personally, I don't like the idea of gambling much. I consider myself to be either a speculator or an investor, not a gambler. When I first started investing, I didn't know the difference (though I started at 18 and had no-one to guide me).

That meant that all my investments were gambles. Mostly, they weren't so hot.

These days, I assess and analyse much more. I avoid 'turnarounds', since I don't think they turn around too often. Greater life experience has taught me to recognise that most companies that need to turn, or might turn, are already dead - they just don't know it yet.

I also have learned my lesson with 'development' companies. You know the thing, one great idea that 'if' they get to market will make 'tens of millions'. I own shares in a couple that I bought years ago.

Broadly, I was right to buy. Of all the development stocks I could have bought, these actually did develop and do make products. They just don't make profits yet - years after I bought.

One of my development picks actually dominates the bluetooth market. That's right, I invested in the company that developed much of the bluetooth technology we use today! How could it not make a bundle of money? Am I a genius or what? Years later, I am still down 65%.

Another has an amazing fuel saving device for gear boxes in cars, lorries and off-road vehicles. In this age, you'd think that fuel saving technology would be all the rage. Over the years, I have bought more shares in the lows and sold them in the highs to make some 'trading' profits. But still my initial investment (I think 8 years ago) is down.

Though I may not have realised it at the time, these were not investments, they were gambles. So is the stock exchange really a place for beginners?

An investment is in a company that has products, a defined market and notable market share, profits, a track record and much more. Remember that. Think about Warren Buffett - he makes investments, good ones at that.

I'm also quite traditional about investing. I have never spread bet, used an option or future or sold short. I don't use leverage. If I can't figure out what might go wrong, FOR CERTAIN, I'd rather not do it. I buy, I hold and I sell. That's it.

I have no doubt that these admissions mean that I miss out on all sorts of possible investment opportunities. There are all sorts of weird and wonderful investments out there, but I invest and I don't like to gamble.

If you think about it though, what I just said doesn't really hold me back. I own some coins, stamps, comics, unit funds, shares, books and art - I did mention that I speculate didn't I? And if the world suddenly has a crisis, it means that I own actual, physical assets as well as just share certificates.

So that brings me to another point ... can you focus?

Ideally, you need to know quite a lot about certain areas and use that knowledge for your investment benefit. The art and books I own are mostly related to cricket. I love cricket and know a lot about the game and it's history - which means that I know when I see something of value.

If it has value now, it probably will have for some time to come. Whether I buy at a good price or not, value and scarcity count.

Who'd imagine ME telling you that the stock market isn't everything?

Investment risk is lowered by knowledge. Every time. If you are buying shares on the stock exchange, what does the seller know that you don't? What do you know that the seller does not?

You can bet your life that the buyer or seller opposite you in any transaction has done some serious research. If you don't do yours, who do you think will win? You or the market?

But the great thing about investment is that in the long run, you decide whether you'll be successful or not. The harder you work at it, the luckier you will be. If you are just starting out, think about YOU first, not the market or companies.

Decide on what you want to specialise on, whether the stock market for beginners is a place to invest and how you will approach it.

It might help to find areas in which you have useful knowledge already. Either that or decide on an area and slowly become an expert. What do I mean? Well, if you worked in a bank for 10 years, you must know something about banking.

When you read an annual report from a bank, do you laugh and see through the waffle or does it make real sense? If you can see through the waffle of some far off CEO and CFO, you can start to compare the relative prospects in the same market of competing firms. Hey - that could be an opportunity!

If you really know about banking, you can compare the product offerings and service as well as the annual reports. You might still know some bank staff that are happy to tell you honestly that they are being 'creamed' in the market or whatever.

Before you know it, you have a picture building of a competitive market. Before long, you will REALLY understand the investment potential of several companies. That will put you far ahead of many other investors.

As I said earlier, investment risk is lowered by knowledge - EVERY TIME.

CHAPTER 2

How to Identify Turnaround stocks

Investing in the stock market is one of the more difficult endeavors to engage in, but it doesn't have to be as hard as you may think. One way to increase your chances of success in the stock market is to search for and invest in turnaround stocks

Finding these gems isn't as difficult as you may think, and that's what I'm going to talk about in this chapter.

More often than not, a company may go through a series of a horrible bankruptcy, which can lead to a major restructuring, or resulting to another company buying it at a great value. Perhaps, the company may turn things around from huge amounts of debt or it has some capital equipment, inventory, patents, real estate, or other forms of assets that have huge sentimental value to the acquirer.

Therefore, if you become careful and conduct a thorough value analysis, you are likely to find a turnaround company that has the potential of being listed on a top exchange.

That said, you have to be careful when investing in penny stocks. Even though, the stock may have a great price and appears to have a great potential of doubling or tripling your investment, you have to be calm and careful.

Do your own research. This way, you will ensure that you earn some good money after sticking to value investing.

Making money in the stock market is usually mostly about recognizing value. Value usually doesn't have much to do with whether a company is a good company or a bad company.

Sometimes excellent companies have overpriced stock that you should therefore not purchase because there is no value in doing so.

On the other hand, however, a company that is not such a great company may have outstanding growth potential that is not factored into the current stock price which means even a small turn around calculates into larger than average stock price increases under certain circumstances... hence it may be a valuable stock.

So how do you find companies with undervalued stock prices that are poised for a quick jump? It is much easier than you think!

First look for stocks that are currently resting at new lows within a 12 to 14 month period. Also look for companies that have a higher probability of being liquidated or are even in the process of liquidation at the moment. Sometimes a company is worth more after it has been liquidated than its current share price reflects.

Next watch out for companies that have recently attempted mergers unsuccessfully. If one company is interested in merging with that company, others may be as well and just because the merger didn't go through the first time doesn't mean other candidates won't follow through completely.

Next look for companies that have recently eliminated their dividend payout, or even companies that have just reduced their dividend payout. Many times when this happens shareholders freak out and sell the stock, which depresses the stock price sometimes further down then it should... which creates a buying opportunity once the stock settles to a more realistic price.

There you have several ways to find depressed stock prices that have a fairly good chance of making a sudden increase or turnaround. As with all investing opportunities, be sure to do thorough research before making a final investment decision.

Buy penny stocks if you want to invest in the stock market. The stock market is very risky right now. No one knows what is going to happen with the economy and so investing in stocks with a quick turnaround profit is the way to go.

Day trading to gain money in your pocket now is best when the future is so uncertain. It is highly risky, but that also makes it highly profitable.

The fact that you can buy penny stocks for $5 a share or under, makes investing in them very desirable. It allows people with a wide range of income to buy them. It can be a great place to start as a beginner, just make sure to start slowly.

Research a great deal about how to buy stocks before you start investing. Treat it like a class, read books, forums, and blogs to gain as much knowledge as you can. Knowledge is key to investing in the stock market, whether you invest in the big companies or the small ones.

Figure out how much you want to invest. How much money would you not mind losing? Of course you want to gain and you can make money, but always be careful when playing the stock market. And remember you can make money, despite what others may have told you.

Don't expect a great deal of money overnight, it will take time to learn everything. Be persistent, patient, and research, research, research. Discover everything about the companies and beware of scams. So learn a lot and have fun when you buy penny stocks.

Finally look for companies that are in financial difficulty but at the same time have shareholders who are larger companies with a stronger balance sheet. Many times if a company has a large shareholder in the same industry or in a similar industry they can infuse capital which should bump up the share price.

Watching Out For the Turnaround

There are many types of investment methodology out there. All of them has their own merits. What is turnaround stocks? They are normally companies that are experiencing problems (hopefully short-term), and a lot of people are not willing to wait for those companies to recover.

I personally like turnaround stocks for two main reasons; First, turnaround stocks have problems in the open. The problem has been disclosed and our task as investor is to figure out how much the company is worth should the problem persists or when the problem goes away.

Granted, there might be more problems discovered along the way. But at the very least, some of the problems has come out and the share price generally has dropped because of that.

Secondly, expectation is low for turnaround investment. Share price is already depressed due to known problems. The company does not have to 'beat expectation' every time it reports earning. All it has to do is clear out the problems that causes its stock price to drop on the first place.

It's the oldest and most important rule in investment - buy low, sell high. So with inventory soaring and housing prices dropping, many people out there are wondering when's the best time to buy a new home? Here are a few signs to look out for if you want to know just when the market is about to turn around.

Keep in mind that real estate is local. What is happening in one market may not necessarily reflect changes in another market. If home prices are turning around in Texas, that doesn't mean we're there yet here in Central Florida. So pay attention to the local market when looking out for these signs.

One of the most important things to look out for is changes in the local job market. Higher unemployment, of course, leads to fewer potential home buyers and even more homes added to the market as people move to more job-rich areas and try to get out from under their mortgage payments.

High unemployment also leads to more foreclosures, raising housing inventory even higher and dropping prices even lower. Watch for a sudden surge of new jobs being created in an area. Maybe a new resort is going up, bringing in construction jobs and the need for service workers.

A new factory, a town center, or a whole new community can all lead to an upsurge in jobs and in nearby housing prices.

Watch the housing stock in your area. It's simple supply and demand - when you see the amount of houses on the market start shrinking, the demand is getting higher and prices will soon be on the rise again. The sale of homes is a seasonal thing, people tend to buy property more at certain times of the year, so don't compare the numbers from one month to the next, compare them to the same month from a year ago. Your real estate agent can help compile and read these statistics. When the housing stock starts to shrink and the prices start to rise, you'll know we've gone around the corner.

It's also a good sign when the average price of homes starts falling at a slower pace. Even as prices continue to drop, watch the rate of descent. If the rate starts to slow, prices are leveling off and we're nearing the bottom.

Again, talk to your agent about this. Because real estate figures can vary drastically depending on the season, it's best to get a wide timeframe of statistics so that you can see trends more easily.

Find out the rent-to-own ratio in your area. The math is pretty simple. Find out how much it would cost to buy a home, then talk to your real estate broker and find out how much it would be to rent a similar property.

Divide the two to get your rent-to-own ratio. Normally, a good ratio would be around 15 or lower but this can vary somewhat depending on the market you're in. In the first few months of 2008, the rent-to-own ratio in Orlando was 22.2, already down from the peak ratio of 26.7 and continuing to drop.

Finally, check the affordability of homes in your area. The National Association of Home Builders keeps what it calls the "housing opportunity index" - a list of affordability levels in hundreds of metro areas.

A home is considered affordable if 28% or less of the median family income for the area is required to pay for it. Nationally, the average is 53.8, meaning that slightly more than half of the homes in the area are considered affordable. In Orlando, the rate is 48.1 currently, a little less than half.

Again, since real estate is more local, it might be useful to compare this number to the affordability rate of past years rather than comparing it with the national average. Your agent should be able to help you find these figures. When affordability rates start going up, the housing market is turning around.

Once we hit the bottom, buyers in Central Florida will find themselves faced with a huge buying opportunity. We may not be there yet, but we can see it getting closer and closer. Some of the signs are already starting to show.

Our stock of homes is shrinking slowly but surely. The affordability rate is continuing to go down. New employment opportunities are around the corner with new projects and communities going up, including Florida Hospital's ambitious 172 acre Health Village scheduled to start construction next year!

We're nearing the bottom and you're going to want to already be looking up when we get there!

How should one find a potential turnaround candidates for their portfolio? The one thing that I found useful is to read the financial news. Companies that are in trouble can be easily spotted in the news.

For example, this week brought news from Pier 1 Imports Inc. (PIR) and Doral Financial (DRL). Are these companies in trouble? Sure. Are they turnaround candidates? Possibly.

Another good source would be the list of stocks that are touching 52 week low. Most of these lists would be companies that are experiencing problems and hence has the potential of turning around. For example ATI Technologies Inc. (ATYT) trade closes to its 52 week low of $ 11.20.

What to avoid when sifting through lists of potential turnaround investment? I would avoid company that is getting hammered due to the delay in its financial reporting. No matter how low the share price is, investors do not and should not invest in companies that has some trust issues.

Once we identify our target, we can then do some analysis to determine the fair value of the stock. There are chances that some companies may never recover. So, we have to take that into accounts when doing fair value calculation.

Calculating fair value is a whole brand new topic and I won't get into the details here. But obviously, a stock will have a higher fair value if it can recover from current problems than a stock that cannot overcome its current problems.

Turnaround stock trading is not for the faint of heart or the unprepared. If turnaround stocks are anything, they are extremely volatile. On the other side of that coin, they can be amazingly profitable if you know how to manage high risk. It's all a matter of knowing what you are doing.

Turnaround stocks are very similar to standard stocks other than the fact that they are not traded on the major stock exchanges. Turnaround stocks are, by definition, stocks that are trading at or below five dollars a share. The purpose of trading these stocks is just the same as regular stocks: Try to buy low and then sell high.

Turnaround stocks are a lot more volatile than standard stocks and this is both their significant advantage AND their foremost disadvantage. These stocks are known to double their value in only one day whereas it could take weeks, months or even years for a normal stock to do likewise.

The truth is it is a lot easier for a stock priced at a penny per share to increase its worth to two pennies per share than it is for a stock worth thirty dollars a share to double its price to sixty dollars a share.

How all of this impacts the turnaround stock investor is a good news/bad news type of thing. Bad news first: Turnaround stocks can be so volatile that you are able to lose your total investment in no more than a single trading day. It's not remarkable for a stock worth a penny a share to go to zero quickly.

Normal stocks are able to also go to zero but they will spend a much longer period doing it, offering the investor a chance to sell his or her position and hold onto a portion of his or her capital.

You can rapidly be blind-sided by turnaround stocks if you are not watching closely with your finger ready on the sell trigger. These stocks don't always perform as you would guess after investigating the books of a company. In the universe of turnaround stocks, one often sees good companies going down and bad companies going up.

The good news? You are able to make a gigantic percentage increase quickly with only a conservative amount of capital at risk. And, while you can lose nearly all or all of your capital quickly, you won't be injured that much if you have only involved a small part of your entire net worth. Obviously, investing just a penny today and then having two pennies tomorrow is not apt to change your life that much, so you may be tempted to try to double a much more sizeable initial investment.

Because of the volatility of these stocks, you should never put in more than you can afford to lose.

How, then, can you put the odds in your favor? It's all about selecting the perfect turnaround stock and you may want some help there. Use professional stock picks from a reliable stock-picking service for a start.

Make a list of the 10 best turnaround stocks from the stock picking service and then do your own research.

List these ten stocks on a spreadsheet and make columns for company earnings, book value and such.

As said above, turnaround stocks do not continually work out as you might guess from the company books but most of the time they do, therefore going through the above exercise is not without value.

Listing the 10 stocks on a spreadsheet helps you see easily which one of them is most likely going to be a winner. After placing your buy order, keep a journal of the exact outcomes of all 10 stocks, including the ones you decided not to buy. This will be a wonderful learning exercise for you.

Profit from your past mistakes. Try to understand what went wrong and why. Don't commit the same errors again. Observe what other investors are doing and learn from their ups and downs.

If the price of a stock is low, plan to find out if it is because it has not yet been discovered or if, rather, the corporation is in financial trouble. Buy the first never the second.

If it happens that you have a sizeable win of one hundred percent or more, it's time to sell all or a portion of your holding in that turnaround stock. There are a few ways to achieve this. You could sell fifty percent of your shares and let the other half ride or, as an alternative, you would leave 1/3 in, sell 1/3 for cash in your pocket and sell then invest the dollar amount of the final third in another, different, turnaround stock. Don't get greedy and hang onto a stock past its time. What goes up must come down and turnaround stocks usually do that quickly.

If the stock keeps ascending after you have dumped it, don't worry about it. There will be another train leaving the station in five minutes. The whole idea is to buy under-valued issues and then sell them before they become over-valued. Never buy or get rid of for emotional reasons. Habitually go by the numbers and stay on your plan.

Finally, be careful about hot turnaround stock tips from promoters. Promoters buy a turnaround stock and then try to prevail on everyone else in the world to buy the same turnaround stock, thus driving the price up.

Since they made their acquisition before you did, they will make a 100% gain or more before you can really profit and will then dump the stock like a hot potato causing an immediate and unexpected decline in share value at your expense.

What To Expect When Buying Turnaround stocks

Stock investing, especially buying turnaround stocks, is not just a get rich quick scheme. This is real business that some of the world's richest and most powerful people use every day to earn a fortune. However, because of the nature of these stocks, one needs to exercise caution coupled with thorough research when investing.

These stocks are often overlooked when it comes to making money with stocks. Some believes that all you have to do is learn how to spot the right pick and take advantage of them.

Investing in these stocks can be pretty exciting as they are the fast movers of the stock market. While large stocks such as IBM and Microsoft lumber along like the giants that they are, buying turnaround stocks come be compared to racing around in a Ferrari.

Investing in these can be a great way to make money fast but it is also a great way to lose money fast. So know exactly how much you are will to risk.

These stocks are cheap for a good reason. Most financial advisors will advise against trading in them because most people lose money, the commissions are huge and they are subject to price manipulation due to the small float. They are also extremely volatile. It's not unusual for such a stock to go up over 50% in 1 day.

Although buying turnaround stocks are considered high risk but they do carry the potential to eventual high reward. That is what makes them so attractive... comparative low investment for quick profit turnaround. For a hundred dollars, you can buy literally thousands of stocks.

This is also why it is important to do extensive market research when dealing with these stocks. It would be great of course if the research can be outsourced to an individual or even a system.

Find out about a newsletter that provides weekly stock picks analyzed by the world's first stock trading robot to assist investors who are buying or thinking of buying turnaround stocks here.

CHAPTER 3

Turnaround investors and patience

Many people profess to be patient investors. In reality, not many can stand the heat of waiting their investments to turn around. You can identify such investors by asking them the reason why they invest on their stocks.

If they said that they invest because such and such has an exciting products in the pipeline, then they are most likely are not going to be patient with that investment.

If they admit that things look gloomy for their investment but, they believe that the company will turn that around with certain new executions, then they are patient investors. The truth is turnaround investors are patient investors.

They are willing to invest in a seemingly gloomy company with the expectation that things will change. No, it is not a stream of baseless hope. It is the patience to wait until the company can sort its mess out.

That is hard to do, even for the most-seasoned turnaround investors. The reason is simple. You invest in companies that people love to hate. You need to have strong conviction in order to stay on the course.

A lot of novice investors would buy some beaten down companies, only to sell it later due to emotional reasons. For instance, one folk might talked unfavorably about your company and you start to think that maybe he was right.

After a while, another folk would talk some other terrifying things about your company and your mind started to tremble. At that point, you could not wait to dump your investments in this stock and you were glad you sold the stock.

That happens a lot and that is the reason why turnaround investors are rewarded so much. Since not a lot of investors are willing to wait that long, the stock price can be bought at a much lower price than normal. This increases your potential return.

What are examples of turnaround investments? Hindsight is 20-20. But, let me give a few examples in the past. Altria Inc. was a good turnaround investment in the early 2000s. It was hit by lawsuits left and right and nobody is willing to buy a stock with 'tobacco' labelled in them.

Fast forward five years later, people still do not have a favorable view on tobacco but Altria stock price increase anyway. It is not a mere penny increase that we are talking about. Altria increases more than 200% since its low price in the year 2000.

How about Seagate Technology in the middle of last year? Analysts worry about the competition from flash disk which would cripple the hard-drive industry forever. The result? Seagate stock price rose almost 100% within one year. Not a bad return for investing in un-loved companies.

One final example would be the pharmaceutical companies. Concerns about their future pipeline depressed their stock price for much of 2005. In 2006, when it is clear that the pipeline is not all dry, stock price rose steadily to reflect that change.

You could have bought Merck shares in the $ 26 range last year and your investment would have gained 36% thus far. This is despite the uncertainty revolving around it. When the vioxx case is all settled, I think the stock price can rise approaching the pre-vioxx announcement.

The key here though is to be knowledgeable about your companies and be patient. This way, you will have a strong conviction about your investment and you will not sell a potentially good investment portfolio. That is not easy to do but you will get better at it with practice.

For starter, our website features a regular commentary that gives you free investing idea about potential turnaround investment.

Practically everyone takes a flawed approach to buying stocks. So, practically everyone ends up with a rotten loss-making portfolio.

But remember... you have to do lots of "donkey" work to become a successful "bull" on the stock markets. You must also have monumental patience and play stocks with a long-term perspective. Hoping to multiply money in quick time is a definite recipe for disaster.

1. First and foremost, you have to understand and appreciate that when you are buying stocks you are NOT buying some symbols on the screen. Instead, you are buying an underlying business.

You are becoming a partner in that business. Therefore, you share its profits and its losses. That is why the term... shareholder.

2. It is but obvious that you have to buy sunrise businesses. If the products and services of any industry are not in demand, it would be foolhardy to become a partner in such businesses.

3. However, quite often, two companies in the "same industry" follow diametrically opposite paths... one profitable and the other losing money. The answer to this oddity lies in the quality of entrepreneurship.

Good managements make good businesses. Bad managements fail frequently. Backing proven managers is, therefore, the most sacrosanct and inviolable principle of investing in stocks.

4. Sometimes even good managements and good businesses go through tough times. Therefore, apart from ascertaining that the company is running a good business and managed by a good team, you have to ensure that it makes good sales and earns good profits.

Never invest in a loss-making company, unless you see strong signs of a turnaround in the near future.

5. Operational performance is one part of the story. The other significant aspect is its financial foundation. All businesses have to withstand the vagaries of the economy. For example, too much debt may not be an issue during good times.

But it can seriously threaten even the existence of the company when economic conditions turn bleak. As such, strong balance sheets always make a dependable choice.

6. Wait... a company with excellent business, excellent management, excellent financial strength and excellent profits, is not the green signal to cut your cheque. No. There is one more critical parameter - its market price.

If the price is too high relative to its underlying valuation, even excellent shares will not make money for you. A reasonable PEG ratio determines a reasonable stock to buy.

This is the safe, sensible and steady approach to buying shares. It would surely give you a lot more winners than losers. And, to succeed you don't need ALL the players to do well. A few good performances, backed by at least average play from others will definitely win you most matches.

CHAPTER 4

Analysis of stocks - A necessity for stock traders

Stock is a category of safety that indicates ownership in a company and symbolizes an assortment on fraction of the corporation's assets and earnings. There are two most important types of stock value: common and favorite.

Common stock frequently entitles the proprietor to make your choice at shareholders' meetings and to obtain dividends. Preferred stock generally does not have voting rights, but has an advanced claim on assets and earnings than the ordinary shares.

For example, owners of preferred stock receive dividends before ordinary shareholders and have precedence in the event that a company goes bankrupt and is settled. The capital stock (or just stock) of a business creature represents the original capital paid into or invested in the business by its founders.

It serves as safekeeping for the creditors of a business since it cannot be withdrawn to the harm of the creditors. Stock market is different from the property and the assets of a business which may alter in quantity and value.

A stock exchange is a body that provides military for stock brokers and traders to trade stocks, bonds, and other securities. Stock exchanges also provide conveniences for question and deliverance of securities and other economic instruments, and capital events including the payment of income and dividends.

Securities traded on a stock exchange include shares issued by companies, unit trusts, derivatives, mutual investment products and bonds. The stock of a business is divided into multiple shares, the sum of which has to be stated at the time of business arrangement.

Given the total amount of money invested in the business, a share has a definite declared face charge, generally known as the equivalence value of a share. The stock prices are the price of a solitary share of a number of profitable stocks of a company. Once the stock is purchased, the owner becomes a shareholder of the company that issued the share. The par value is the least (minimum) amount of money that a business may concern and sell shares for in many jurisdictions and it is the value represented as capital in the accounting of the business.

In other jurisdictions, however, shares may not have an associated par value at all. Such stock is often called non-par stock. Stock picks are methods for selecting a stock(s) for investment.

The stock investment or location can be "long" (to benefit from a stock price increase) or "short" (to benefit from a decrease in a stock's price), depending on the investor's expectation of how the stock price is going to move.

The stock collection criterion may include systematic stock picking methods that utilize computer software and/or data. Shares represent a fraction of ownership in a business. A business may declare different types of shares, each having distinguishing ownership rules, privileges, or share values.

Ownership of shares is documented by issuance of a stock certificate. A stock certificate is a lawful document that specifies the amount of shares owned by the shareholder, and other particulars of the shares, such as the equivalence worth, if any, or the course group of the shares.

In economic markets, stock value is the technique of manipulative academic values of companies and their stocks.

The most important draw on of these methods is to forecast prospect market prices, or more normally possible market prices, and accordingly to earnings from price association - stocks that are judged undervalued (with respect to their academic value) are bought.

While stocks that are judged overvalued are sold, in the likelihood that undervalued stocks will, on the complete, rise in value, while overestimated stocks will, on the complete, go down.

CHAPTER 5

Technical analysis

Global recession has undercut through the fault lines of Indian stock markets. FII are selling off the bourses and it has brought the stocks to a virtual landslide. Stocks with high-held head at 22000 are looking for safe nooks at around the 8000 levels.

Market capitalization is at abysmal low and to add to the trauma, global cues are not getting any stronger.

In these dark times it becomes even more important to rummage through the technical analysis section of BSE/NSE before trading, investing or even speculating (we mean the quintessential day traders) Technical analysis is the method of stock analysis either perfected by a stock expert or unassuming software with potential of grasping market clues.

Technical analysis software's can help a trader in exploiting the BSE and NSE for their diverse day trading and investment opportunities. These can be charting modules which align to methods of technical analysis and stock analysis. The software also helps in drafting the candlestick patterns.

What's more! The software provides terminus for trading in NSE listed stock and the unpredictable futures trading. Let's forget about the "too technical" aspect of technical analysis and center our thoughts on the largely fundamental plane. All of us know of the present market volatility in Indian market.

It is funny how the 'resistance lines' are falling apart and 'corrections' have become elusive. We see 'rallies' but they are largely negative runs. 'Circuits' have become a common site given the consistently sorry hours of trading.

In such times, stock investment needs a lot of grit and heart of steel but it also needs prior technical analysis advices. Technical analysts may look for Fibonacci retracements and other technical dropdowns but they assist us in fundamental, layman based way. Technical analysis talks about the largely expected direction of stock movement and recommends stop losses ands stop profits in advance.

Technical analysis endorsements can enable a layman to decide whether to buy/hold/sell his stock. Such portfolio management by experts can yield great fruit in the long run.

The stock analysis methods can help a novice to understand the precision exit points for winning stocks. This way he can fully maximize sharp turns of a fledgling market. The analysts track the stocks a person wishes to venture into, and then suggest precision entry levels.

Technical analysis also teaches us the techniques of derivative training and asks us to make profit both while the stocks fall and the stocks rise. There are groups providing high-class equity services.

These provide new wave automated online services allowing the traders to become members and set their own terminuses. Panels of experts and technical analysis folks help in analyzing over 200 BSE scripts.

The online trading system permits a trader to pursue the market through aligning to market watch, research tip receipt, stock alerts and real-time charts and news. The sites also ask you to trade any time-frame and generate few viable trading pips for you. All these can help one trade in these tough times.

Warren Buffet recently bought a lot of stocks on the falling Wall Street bourse. He proclaimed prophetically that "stocks is about being fearful when all else are greedy and being greedy when all else are fearful"

Here are a few things you can look at.

1. The P/E ratio

Everyone looks at the P/E ratio. It helps you to get an understanding of how the price of the stock compares with the actual earnings of the company which is of course the lifeblood of the company. To find the P/E ratio you divide the price of the stock with the earnings per share.

For example say a stock is trading at $30 and has an earnings per share of $2 the P/E ration would be 15. Well now that you know how to figure it out how can you tell if it is good or bad? You need to compare it with other companies; the lower the P/E is the better.

So if the average company in that industry group has a p/e ratio of 25 then a p/e of 15 means the company is greatly undervalued. If the average p/e ratio is 10 well then a p/e of 15 means the stock is probably undervalued compared to others.

2. PEG ratio

The PEG ratio is another way for you to look at the p/e ratio. To find this you simply divide it by earnings growth. The good thing about this is it can tell you faster weather the company is overvalued or undervalued.

If the PEG is below 1 it is said to be a good undervalued and therefore a good buy. If it is over 1 it is said to be overvalued and therefore a bad buy.

3. Debt to Capital Ratio

It is very important to figure out the debt of a company. You don't want to buy a company that has too much debt because if might not be able to pay it off. This ratio is simply how much of a company's total capital is borrowed money. The less the better.

Predicting movements in the currency market is no easy matter and traders need to decide on a method for analyzing the market to underpin their trading decisions. Today analysts are divided into two main groups; fundamental analysts and technical analysts.

Two Methods For Analyzing Movements In The Forex Market

In many ways the Forex, foreign exchange or foreign currency market is no different from any other market and prices are driven largely by the simple laws of supply and demand. If a currency is in demand its price will rise, but if demand is low its price will fall.

This principle is fairly simple to understand and you might think that, against this background, it should be quite easy to predict movements in currency prices. Unfortunately, this is not the case.

Up until the mid 1980s the majority of traders relied on a method known as fundamental analysis to predict movements in the market.

Today however an increasing number of traders have turned away from fundamental analysis in favor of technical analysis, although there are still a significant number of traders who have stuck with fundamental analysis, or who use it to back up the results of their technical analysis.

Let's take a brief look at each of these two analytical methods.

Fundamental Analysis

The principle behind fundamental analysis is that it is changes in political, economic and social factors which dictate supply and demand and movements in the market can be predicted by studying these factors.

Fundamental analysis thus looks at political events and economic data such as inflation, interest rates and trade figures, as well as social data such as employment rates. Historical data is then used as the basis for predicting movements in the light of current figures.

In other words an analysis of, for example, the effect that rising or falling interest rates have had on currency prices in the past is used to predict the effect that a rise or fall in rates today will have.

The greatest problem with fundamental analysis lies in the huge quantity of data which needs to be analyzed and in the fact that there is a wide degree of disagreement over which data is important and which is not.

It is also felt in some quarters that since the world has changed dramatically in recent years many of the factors which may have affected currency prices in the past will not necessarily have the same effect today.

Perhaps one area of general agreement however is that analysis of a country's balance of payments is crucial to the success of fundamental analysis.

The balance of payments is important because it reflects the flow of currency in and out of a country and a situation in which money is flowing into a country faster than it is flowing out, or vice versa, will clearly affect currency prices.

Analyzing just how prices will be affected is of course something which is hotly debated by fundamental analysts.

Technical Analysis

The principle behind technical analysis is simply that, while political, economic and social factors will indeed drive the market, it is not necessary to study, or even to understand, these because these factors in whatever combination you choose have occurred time and again in the past and their affect can be seen by simply studying the historical pattern of currency movements.

Accordingly, the main tool of the technical analyst is the chart, or more accurately a series of charts, which provides a graphical representation of the market over time.

A study of such charts will show that there are clear trends and patterns to price movements and so extending a current chart on the basis of past patterns will show the direction in which a currency will move.

As with fundamental analysis, there is a wide range of different charting tools available and widespread disagreement over which are valuable and which are of lesser or little use.

Should You Choose Fundamental Or Technical Analysis

Deciding which method you should adopt is no easy matter, although most novice traders today choose to follow technical analysis.

This could of course be because they firmly believe that this is the better of the two methods but, it is probably because learning the skills of fundamental analysis takes a great deal of time and involves a steep learning curve and because this is the direction in which Forex trading is moving.

When you buy stocks, it is important to take a look at the profit and loss trends with that stock. If they drop more than they climb during day trading, then you're taking a risk. The profits may be great at one time, but not selling at the right time could result in significant losses. You want to know when the right time to sell is.

Another reason why you may wish to watch stock trends is because you want to buy low and sell high. Stock trends always show what the lowest trading price and what the highest trading price has been during day trading.

That way, you know it is time to sell if your stock has reached or exceeded the highest trading price listed. Some individuals decide to sit on that stock despite the high sale price, but could be risking not getting the maximum out of their stock.

However, by monitoring stock trends and news surrounding that stock and its company, those individuals can make an informed decision as to whether or not to sit on it or whether or not to sell.

Power of trend lines

It doesn't matter if you are a high risk individual or one who does not like risk at all, monitoring the stock trends are very important. If you are not a risky person or you are unable to keep a steady eye on stocks that fluctuate quickly, you may want to buy stock that doesn't have rapid fluctuations.

If you look at the trends of the stock market as a whole, you will see that it can rise at a very high speed, but it can also drop at the same speed or faster. However, what you will notice by studying the trend lines is the fact that when it is down it always goes back up.

This seems to be what we have been seeing in the stock market in recent days, but this can always change. However, stock trends can certainly tell you a story about the stocks that you are investing in and whether or not you want to invest in that stock.

Basically, trend lines more or less take care of the guess work when you buy stocks. You shouldn't have to guess with your money if you don't have to. When some individuals lose money on stock and they say that they wish someone would have told them about that stock, they obviously didn't look at the stock trends.

The stock trends tells them whether or not they should use as much as a ten foot pole to touch that stock with, let alone invest large sums of money in it. Sure, it may be great to buy that stock when it goes down, but the trends will display whether or not that stock will move up when it goes down.

This takes up back to the aspect of buying when stock is low and selling when it is high.

By buying low on a stock that shows trends of bouncing back can be quite profitable. A stock that has consistently bounced back after reaching very low prices shows that the stock is very resilient.

If it currently shows that the stock is dropping and dropping fast, it is important to watch it. If past trend lines show that it always bounces back, then this stock may be worth investing in.

However, you must evaluate how quickly the stock climbs after it has dropped and determine when you want to sell based on the trends.

If it is prone to dropping quickly, then you may want to sell when it reaches a price comparable to its highest trading price according to the trend lines. With this, it is very obvious how powerful trend lines are in deciding how profitable you can be.

Monitoring stock trends

It is important to not be lazy when monitoring stock trends since they help you determine when to buy stocks and sell stocks. But we all live busy lifestyles that can make it difficult to constantly research and monitor our stocks.

That is why a stock screener presents a great solution. What a stock screener will do is notify you of any trading signals, provide you with strategies, show you charts that notify you of the trends your stocks are experiencing, and will notify you of hot stock picks. The hot stock picks are based upon the overall performance of that stock based on your risk level and other criteria. Basically, a stock screener is allowing you to optimize your stock trades and use investment strategies that will give you the best return on your investment.

A stock screener such as Technical Stock Screener provides you with all of the information needed to be successful in your stocks.

A stock screener puts all of your stock information in one place so that you do not have to tediously search market listings throughout the internet or, if you wish to buy stocks, you are not trying to find the best stock picks on your own.

It is easy to miss the best stocks when you are trying to find them on your own and it isn't your fault. It is simply because it is difficult to sift through all of the stocks on the market to find the best one. It can also take up time that you don't have.

That is why there is a stock screener to help you identify those important stock trends to help you decide when the best time to make a move with your stocks is. What you will find is that you can maximize your investment by being better informed about the happenings of the market.

CHAPTER 6

Stock Market Facts & Fiction

Millions of Americans invest in the stock market directly and many millions more invest in the stock market indirectly by owning mutual funds in 401k plans, IRAs and so on. Most don't really understand their stock investment, and some are just clueless. Where do you fit? Here's a morsel of stock market fact and some fiction.

The stock market goes up more often than it goes down... That's a fact, and the reason stock investing has interested people for decades. However, the market goes through cycles that are difficult to foresee ahead of time. In other words, there are good times in the stock market and there are bad times.

People should invest money in stocks primarily to receive dividends... I call that fiction because the primary source of profits in stock investing comes from price appreciation. That's a fancy term for rising stock prices.

Some of the best stock investments over the years have paid virtually no dividends at all. They are commonly called growth stocks. If you pay $10 for a stock and sell it a few years later for $50, who needs dividends?

"Equities" is another term for stocks, and unless you have big bucks you can not invest money in them... Equities are stocks, they go by both names. Unless you consider a couple of thousand dollars a lot of money, the rest of the statement is not true. However, if you can not afford to take a loss do not make a stock investment.

The stock market pays 10% a year... Watch out for that one. Over the years equities have returned on average 10% over the long term. Last decade the average stock investment actually lost money.

Stocks PAY about 2% yearly in dividends on average. When the stock market goes down over a period of years, these dividends help; but they won't save you from taking a loss.

Equity mutual funds are a safe form of stock investing... If you don't have the knowledge or experience or inclination to manage a portfolio of equities on your own, they are your best stock investment. But you don't invest in them for safety. You invest for growth, to earn a higher return.

When you invest money with a financial planner, part of his job is to assure you make money in any stock investment he puts you into... Unless his or her name is Houdini, you're asking too much.

A financial planner's job is to help you reach your financial goals as you expressed them to him. When the market's down, the vast majority of people lose money in their stock investment. Period.

If the stock market falls 50%, and then goes up 50% you break even... Not quite. Ask those who were into stock investing in 2008 through 2009. If a $1000 stock investment falls 50% it is worth $500. If it then goes up 50% you've got $750. Learn to think in terms of percentages. Taking a big loss can set you back for years.

The best stock is often a penny stock... The greatest percentage gainers are often low- price issues, and can go up 1000% or more in a year.

However, as a group they are very risky and not your best stock investment. If you pay less than $1 a share and the share price drops to zero, you've lost 100%, no matter how much you had invested. The majority of true penny stocks get cheaper and then disappear, worthless.

If everything in this article was obvious to you, you are obviously not clueless when it comes to stock investing.

On the other hand, I like to write on a real basic level once in a while, because I've learned that most people don't understand the basics when they invest money. It's better to pick up a morsel of facts once in a while than to continue to invest money totally uninformed.

It's the fiction that can ruin your financial future if you don't know the difference. Especially if a scam artist gets your name and telephone number.

Beating the stock market consistently is a very low-probability proposition. Very few professional investors can do it. The good news is that you do not need to beat the market to make money stock investing. But you do need to learn to separate fact from fiction.

CHAPTER 7

Importance of Financial Analysis

Analysis of stocks, or stock analysis, is something which any stock market trader or investor must master. The purpose of trading the stock market or of investing is to make money.

When the market or individual stock is in an upward movement it is quite simple for anyone to make money by purchasing good stocks, then holding them while prices continue to move up.

They must be sold of course before the uptrend turns down or immediately thereafter. You should not expect to buy at the bottom and sell exactly at the top of the uptrend. You will with care be able to take advantage of part of the upward movement of the stock.

The trap which must be avoided is that of holding on for too long as you wait for the uptrend to reach its top. The market has a habit of turning down very sharply, and in nearly no time at all you may lose all of the profits you have on paper.

A great many people see their stocks turn down, and then hang on expecting this to be a short correction followed by continuation of the uptrend. All too often this is not the case.

A good knowledge of analysis of stocks, and of market trends, is very necessary for anyone who desires to profit from the stock market. Stock analysis is really an art as much as a skill.

Certain individuals have a natural aptitude for stock analysis and can confidently pick good stocks to buy. They also have a well calculated picture of when to sell their stocks for a profit.

It is unfortunately true nevertheless that many people involved in stock trading do not have the necessary stock analysis skills, or the right mindset for success in the stock market. People have a tendency to form an emotional attachment to a stock once they have acquired it.

They form mentally a price objective for the stock and believe, despite any evidence to the contrary, that the stock will survive any downturn and will very soon move up to their selling point. It is very easy to watch a stock till it drops in price to below where you purchased it.

Now the decision is whether to take a small loss, or to hang on doggedly while hoping that the stock will reverse the down move and turn into an uptrend once more.

The unrealised small loss very quickly become a much bigger loss and you are forced to sell the stock as it continues to move down. To avoid such fatal errors the necessary skills in both technical and fundamental analysis of stocks must be acquired. The way to success is to study the market and to read good books you can obtain on this subject.

It is a necessity to develop solid trading skills which are backed by market knowledge and by study of its history. Events which have taken place before in the market always repeat themselves.

A bull market will last for some time, then it will inevitably turn down into the subsequent bear market. This has always been how events unfold and the markets will continue to act in this way. As a stock trader or investor you must never become attached to a stock. If you do you will probably hold on to it for too long and lose money as a result.

Emotions should take no part in trading the stock market. Buying or selling must always be the result of an objective decision which is based on the facts. If you find that you cannot maintain a steely hard objective outlook on the market you would be well advised to stay out of it or you will lose money.

Analysis of stocks based on facts and figures is the basis for sound stock market trading and investing. Before buying it The stock must be analysed to ensure that it has solid fundamentals. The market trend and the trend of the stock itself must be confirmed using technical analysis of stock charts.

Technical analysis is an art which must be learned by study of the technical facts involved in trading stocks, and the patterns they tend to form on charts.

The market may be trending strongly upward but a stock may turn down due to fundamental problems in the company or even due to investor sentiment which has turned away from what was a popular stock in favor another investment.

Financial analysis is done by financial analysts to assess the profitability, stability and viability of a business or organization. Financial analysts use various tools and techniques to conduct financial analysis.

Nowadays outsourcing has become a common practice for many companies. Financial analysis can also be outsourced. Outsourcing financial analysis can be a low cost way of conducting financial analysis.

Many companies may not be able to do a financial analysis of their own company by themselves as it can be difficult to analyze the financial position of your company just by looking at the financial statements.

Financial analysts have a look at the assets and liabilities of the company and many other aspects and decide the company's strengths and weaknesses. Financial analysis for a company also helps in making a comparison with other companies in the same industry.

Outsourcing can have many advantages for companies. Many different streams are outsourced nowadays including IT, logistics, manufacturing, etc. While outsourcing would mean reduced overhead and operational costs, it also has some disadvantages such as the risk of exposing confidential data.

When you outsource part of your work to another company, you might have to share confidential data as part of the work. Some firms may not be ready for this. Sometimes people in your own organization may not be competent enough to handle some tasks and carry out the job, so outsourcing becomes a must. By outsourcing financial analysis, you can hire financial analysts outside of your company who are skilled and experts in their fields.

Outsourcing has advantages because you are giving the job to people who have experience and expertise in handling that task as you may not have people with the same skill sets in your company.

Tasks are outsourced to those people or organizations which are specialized in that field which means the job can be completely swiftly with better quality output.

Financial analysts assess the past performance of the company and make comparisons with other similar firms. Using data and techniques, they can determine the value of a company and also make an analysis of future performance.

Financial analysis can help a company to improve its financial position. It is very important to understand the financial health of your company. Financial analysts evaluate the financial health of your company and help you to make the required changes to your company.

Financial analysts can guide companies and individuals to make proper investment decisions. So, whether you decide on outsourcing financial analysis or do it any other wayScience Articles, know that financial planning and analysis is important and can help you grow your business in the right direction.

It can help your company to avoid making major investment mistakes and generate profits.

CHAPTER 8

How to Manage Your Money When Trading Turnaround stocks

Trading turnaround stocks can be enjoyable, exciting and rewarding. Though, lacking proper money management, it could bust your account. Learn how to manage your money before you produce a live trade.

Turnaround stocks can be a really rewarding form of investment if you realize what you are doing and, most significantly, if you control your money properly. Improper money management can destroy your investing account swiftly.

You can get familiar with everything there could be to learn about investing in turnaround stocks, and yet, never be successful because you didn't adhere to the foundations intended to guard the cash in your account.

Firstly, you must never overtrade your account. Trading a huge amount of your account on any one trade is a terrible concept. If the trade fails and you cannot get out of it in time, too much of your account might be lost. You'll soon find yourself coming up with money to fund the account again.

A great rule of thumb is never to endanger greater than a tenth of the account on any trade. By doing that, you are able to lose 10 trades consecutively until you need to subsidize your account once more.

It is not likely that you are able to go down that many trades successively, but it really is a rule that can make it easier to keep the account in place and afford you a lot of stock trading before you get into excessive misfortune.

An even better rule of thumb is never to chance over 5 percent of your account on a single trade. At that rate, your account can sustain lots of bad trades before it is washed-out. No doubt, lesser accounts may not be able to produce trades at that small of a percentage, but as the account grows, make sure you try for that. That will mean risking only $50 on a $1000 account. That is pretty intelligent trading and it will keep you active a long time.

The desire to trade higher portions of an account is overwhelming with turnaround stocks. That may be because it can be a whole lot quicker to run into a big, profitable trade. You possibly can double, triple, quadruple your account or even more on a particular trade in one day.

You still should always work your trading as a business and abide by the principles like you would any business. A trade that can be that lucrative -- one which can double your money or more -- may also come out being that disastrous. The last thing you need is for any trade to put you out of business and make you have to begin anew.

CHAPTER 9

Is Turnaround stock Investing worth it?

Merchandising in stocks is a very prevalent manner of investing and has been around since the 12th century. You may have heard investing in turnaround stocks is full of risk, notwithstanding Investing in any company in general is precarious.

This is business even so if you are going to be trading in the penny market you have to make yourself prehensile about every company to steer clear of the imposition, rip offs, pump and dumps, and other schemes to alienate you from your agonizing earned chips.

Without a bare understanding of the stocks you will be investing in you will make boundless mistakes out of confoundment and absence of direction.

Most turnaround stocks are accustomedly traded on either the 'OTCBB' exchange (over the counter bulletin confiture) or on what is called the 'Pink Sheets'.

OTC markets can be part of the NASDAQ which is the National Association of Securities Dealers Automated Quotation. OTCBB stocks combine national, regional, and foreign equity issues, warrants, units, American Depository Receipts and Direct Participation Programs.

OTC quotation services (OTCBB, Pink Sheets) assist quotation of unlisted securities. OTCBB issuers that become disregardful in their necessary regulatory filings will have their securities withdrawn from the OTC Bulletin Accelerated.

There are generally inexhaustible potency for the growth of ample sufficiency and this is inordinately mesmerizing

to OTC BB investors. While there is an abstractionism to investing in turnaround stock companies I have found that it is more favorable to invest in companies that are still awaiting their future than companies which have already matured what the future holds for them and are now in decline. Accordingly my advantage in turnaround stock investing! How be it, When it comes to investing in turnaround stocks, there is no doubt that there is a huge insubstantially.

Albeit, with a familiarization of solid information, you are ordained to make the greatest preferences available when it comes to turnaround stock investing affluence. When investing in turnaround stocks you have the possibility to dramatically increase your profits, in any case, you can just as impartially loose your assets quickly.

The bottom line is, though, if you are in the business of turnaround stock investing, you ought to know who has your back. There are multitudinal things to contemplate when it comes to turnaround stock investing or any kind of investing for that matter.

First and foremost, is the cost related such as broker fees or commissions. Because of the phase turnaround stock, you may think that the cost of investing is miniature even so nothing can be further from the truth.

Some brokers indeed charge you more and ask for a big capacity in your account before you're accorded to invest in turnaround stocks. This cost ought to be taken into consideration when it comes to your investing gambit as well as what your long term goals are.

You can mitigate most of the cost associated in turnaround stock investing by self-managing your own account.

Nonetheless, If you are new to the world of investing and acquire the systematics, expenses, fees, and writ the least bit confusing it is nobility to utilize the services of a stock broker that is going to engagement with you every step of the way and enlighten the way things labor at least for the first multitudinal trades you make.

One of the centermost aspects to investing wisely with penny stocks is to know which kinds of turnaround stocks are the right ones for you as well as which sort of a broker is excellent fitted for turnaround stock investing.

As a consequence, I will deal in generalities down a few of the centermost things to

bring to mind and exploit with when it comes to finding or selecting the absolute broker for turnaround stock investing.

What you will appreciate is that majority of brokers are principal broker dealers in this become public of penny stock investing. Nonetheless, one of the essential things you

requisite to begin with is investing in the acceptable broker. Some brokers have unpractical restrictions about turnaround stock investing which makes it very

extravagant to invest in turnaround stocks. So be sure to locate out what their terms are as far as turnaround stock investing before you employ their service.

You can also assume that there are things constituting steps that you can convey to guard that the turnaround stocks that you are investing in are the safest types of penny

stocks procurable. With turnaround stock investing, you can observably see why it is significant to have someone that you can trust to bolster you with funding your transactions. As a consequence, it can be tricky for the everyday person to verify if the penny stock they are adjudging investing in is a ample idea or not. Because of the high gambles associated with investing in the stock market, bounteous investors are looking

for a way of investing their hard cash in a lower riskiness that still rewards you with pretty ample returns over time.

There is a culture pattern to the business that consists of assorted little steps that, when followed customarily, can lead to flourishing investing.

It is my true fixed opinion that those with less than one year's behold investing in individual stocks ought to not even think about investing in turnaround stocks, principally if you haven't found your rhythm with the mid- and large-cap universe albeit.

Third, I never, ever waste my time looking at those turnaround stock companies that are hyped in the multitudinal junk emails I get from websites and promoters that are dedicated to turnaround stock investing. With turnaround stocks do not think for a minute that the game has changed.

Often these promoters have clearly nothing at stake in the turnaround stock company they are promoting. Most assuredly, they are paid by the turnaround stock companies to recommend and circularize them.

Apply vigilance when investing in Turnaround stocks. Sometimes it's discerning not to be the early bird when stock investing, instead wait and see what the day will bring before you take exertion. Study the financials of a turnaround stock company. Much turnaround stock companies will have a negative balance albeit it's the flow of boodle and how they put to use their finances that matters the much.

The great investing opportunities are finding companies that manage to reinvent themselves with huge leaders and auxiliary products.

Apply a devoted absolute interest in the effectiveness of the turnaround stock company you're interested in and obtain out about their track record as this will help stipulate what they can achieve/accomplish with the company. Additionally, you ought to only invest do-re-mi that you are expectant to lose.

Much turnaround stocks are high-gamble investments with decline dealing volumes and finite attention from investors. Nevertheless some turnaround stocks are of higher liability than others. Pink Sheets are the majority chancy with no reporting requirements.

Yet these dangerous, pink sheet stocks give you incredible leverage. The leverage you get with the super subs makes up for them being more fatal.

You may have heard investing in turnaround stocks is venturous. Yes, it is riskful, but High risk means high reward. Trafficking turnaround stocks, while inherently precarious, has some unique benefits.

They do dole out the probability to rise 100%, 200%, or even 1000% in a short period of time.

To win in trafficking turnaround stocks, you ought to obtain the stocks that have the first-class potential, fewest quantify of "red flags", and you have got to also have a game plan that will let you lock in solid profits and cheapen gamble.

Also, if you purchase or sell shares of a abject-volume stock, you run the danger of affecting the price alleged to excess demand or supply. This is an advanced technique that has strict requirements and higher risks.

Alleged to the volatility in turnaround stocks, considerable sums of savings can and have been made by investors willing to draw from the insubstantially. One must also know that the liability's are just as immeasurable as the potential for growth.

Factually, I would say the risks of loss is much considerable than the potential for develop which is why it is certainly critical to only invest with "imperil capital". A major riskiness in turnaround stocks is that they are frequently times de-listed from the OTC BB and are unable to get listed on additional exchange or even re-instated on the OTC BB.

Yet with exceedingly ample research and alleged diligence and the company's experience and structure matter-of-factly unlimited bountifulness can be gained with miniaturized insecurity.

Much of the time the riskiness inherent with turnaround stocks can be finite or mitigated by you knowing what you are doing and knowing how to make it a better investment casualness.

With the correct tools and the absolute familiarity, you gigantically minimize the risk. The more wisdom and behold you get, the less liability you incur. Taking the time to read and research will gigantically minimize turnaround stock investing gambles.

If you do not have the disposition for peril then Stay cast out of these dicey turnaround stock investments. See in retrospect, most people fail when it comes to turnaround stocks as the insubstantially are high and they don't do their home labor or research before jumping the gun or a highly promoted penny stocks.

If you know anything about the standard stock market, then you know that the amount of insecurity that something carries is something that is defined by several things. In fact, every stock can be seen from a different risk vantage point from one lender to the after.

With that said, you can deduce that there are some turnaround stocks that are less fatal than others. In short, you need to ascertain that what you invest in has the danger grit that you can indulge or afford.

The blissful news is that turnaround stocks do extend some flexibility in what riskiness that they provide. So, to pack up, here is what you require to do to stipulate just what your grade of insubstantially embracement is.

Pin down the amount of insecurity that you are willing to appropriate on any penny stock that you invest in. Employment with your financial planner or adviser to verify if the amount of gamble is a practical accommodation for your own financial goals in the long term and short term nail down what danger extent you are comfortable with and the model of turnaround stocks that fits those needs.

When you convey the time to really labor out what your financial gamble fortitude is, you will be better applicable to selecting the appropriate kind of turnaround stocks that you can invest in.

The reality is that having the advantageous inclusion of safety and insubstantially is the biggest factor in investing in turnaround stocks.

Conclusion

Hot turnaround stocks can make you massive profits even if you don't have that much money to trade with. Use caution when trading turnaround stocks, but don't overlook the potential rewards.

Turnaround stock trading and stock trading in general has a simple goal, you want to buy shares of a company at a certain price, and sell them for a larger price later on. You deposit money in an account with a brokerage so you can go online and start buying/selling stock, and start receiving the profits from your trading.

You can buy shares of a company and hold them for as long as you want, a day, a week, a month, years...it's completely open ended. There is also something called day trading, where you buy and sell the stock within a very short period of time. This can be seconds, minutes, hours, or the entire day.

Guess you are ready to jump into the band wagon of investors in turnaround stocks. No more delay, start NOW!!!!